Almost Love

poetry for all who love

Laurel Vera

BookLeaf Publishing
India | USA | UK

Made with ❤ on the BookLeaf Publishing Platform
www.bookleafpub.in
www.bookleafpub.com

Dedication

This book is dedicated to everyone who has felt alone in love.

And to my husband, whose love triumphs over every heartbreak before him.

Preface

This collection of poetry has been inspired by tales of love from unrequited hearts over the last quarter of a century. These poems are about finding love, about losing love and about cherishing the memory of love. You are not alone in love, and this book hopes to help any open hearts heal and move forward. Words have the power to hurt us and to heal us, setting us free, but in the end, these words, my words, are just poetry.

Acknowledgements

The author graciously acknowledges the unwavering support of her mother, who has always encouraged her writing and believed in her greatness. This book could not have come to life without the love and dedication from her husband, who gifted both the space and financial foundation to create freely. A special mention extends to Mrs. Courier, her seventh-grade teacher, whose passionate advocacy for writing helped her discover the power of her own voice. Deep gratitude also goes to Dr. William Nericcio, her college professor, whose vibrant intellect and spirited mentorship inspired a lifelong pursuit of literary and personal discovery. And lastly, these poems would not be possible without the loving embrace of all the friends along the way who witnessed and lived through every Almost Love.

Memory

I'm holding on
To feel the same
As I did
In your arms

A memory
That tears at my heart
Which beats faster
When I think of you

Far away
Your pulse beats
Next to mine
In my memory

La Piscina

I was hoping for someone
When I first saw you
You were swimming in the pool
Sunbathed, Adonis gold and cyan blue

Can't believe you looked at me
Blue eyes piercing through
You know sometimes I think
I'm not as pretty as I seem

You know this is what we came for
Lovin' in the sun
Summer full of romance
When you wanna love someone

You know I waited
Stuck in one place
Searching through crowds for your face
But I had to go
I think that we both know
And it was only for a moment
The love that we made
Just because it didn't last
Doesn't mean it wasn't fate

You know this is what we came for
Lovin' in the sun
Summer full of romance
When you wanna love someone

In The End

When you left in the fall without kissing me
In my head I knew the end, it was meant to be
It didn't make it any easier to watch you go
In my heart I know I won't see you anymore
Keroppi pens and trips down to Mexico
Young summer love
But it dies though when you grow old

Left your mark on my heart though we said goodbye
Told myself it's ok I'll find another guy
Summer came
Summer went
Fall brought you back to me
But in the end we both know it wasn't meant to be
Got my kiss right before you walked away this time
Memories stay but in the end...
Young. Love. Dies.

Lapse

I thought about losing you
Before you were ever mine
If you were ever mine
You were never really mine

How a part of me
Is lost in time
You can't count time
There isn't any time

But your blue eyes
Caught in my stare
And you're sweet skin
Two bodies bared...

I'll go back now
Because I wanted to say
I never needed to say
It's always too much to say

Compression

Compression
Of my heart and thought
See
The space no more
You've cut it out
Or maybe filled it in
No matter which way
You
Changed my structure
Compression
Of our bodies welded
Together as one
We are struggling
To still get closer
When no space is left
Between
Our no longer separate souls

370°

It went all the way around us
And then a little more
A little too tight
Had you reaching for the door
Feeling too trapped
A need to break free
You were able to escape
While almost love
Kept its hold on me

Happy Now

Happy now
But I go back
          When it gets dark

Sunsets trigger me
To chase that old spark

Memories
Clouded by what I wanted them to be
          Not what's real

Is there something left
Between you and me

Happy now
But I go back

Hypocrite

You sit in darkness where love eludes
And shadows come to play
And endless night
Light sparse from stars
I know you're not okay
But who am I
To sit and say,
"Get up and change your ways"
For I too keep
A broken heart
Sheltered from the day

Could You Sleep With Me

Tear my clothes off
Scream at me
Thow me against the wall

We'll have tea in the morning
Call me your queen
And I'll kiss you

My eyes open
A darkness
You don't see

Alone
With you
A fallen angel

Finding despair
In flat coke with lunch
Your face says disgust

With me
I inhale it
And

Wake up
From your life
Into my dream

Could you sleep with me again?

Go And Change

One day I left you
Far far away
The love between us is no more
Now when I see you
All across my face
My empty heart you can see

And every breath between us
I forget again each day
Your memory will not fade

While you forgot
Me I remember
That love is too strong
To tear out of my heart

One day I'll see you
Out of my dreams
A memory passing on the street
And as we move closer
No smile will you see
Things they go and change

And I forgot

You will remember
That love is too long
To go back to the start

Cheers

Cheers to you mate
There isn't much more
I've said all I'll say
To even the score

I'd like to think that
In time we'll be friends
But a friendship with you
Might lead to my end

So enjoy this moment
It's probably our last
If I see you again
I'll be leaving quite fast

Only Ends

Did you know I lost my heart
But then you found me
Gave me hope
And I was praying you saw love in me
Let me go so many times
That now I see
There's no start, only ends to you and me
I walked away
But somehow I'm still here
I looked away
But in my dreams you're everywhere
Did you know I thought that
Fate sent me to you
It wasn't all for naught
This love ache
Became my muse
Put my love away, into something new
Because I know how it ends
It's not me you choose

When You're Done

Fool me with your love
We met too young
I tried to tell you
But the words they never come

Led me on
Was it real or just for fun
You changed my life
From the darkness to the sun

I tried to love you
Wasn't I enough
I acted distant
And I thought you'd call my bluff

I'm so confused
I thought you were the one
You're taken now, but
Call me when you're done

For Us, You're Welcome

You're welcome
For taking a chance or two
When the universe sent me you
When I was your only friend
When I taught you to feel again

You're welcome
When you were counting the days
When you were looking for ways
And then I came through
Reflected the music in you

You're welcome
For standing away
Sitting by, while you played
Said we'd always be friends
Until you learned to love again

But you didn't come back
Just left me alone to unpack
All the hopes that I dreamed
For us
    You're welcome

Days' End

I didn't know that I loved you
Until it was too late
And you'd decided
That you were through
-I was never over you-

You moved on
And what was I to do?
I found a love
And built a life with someone new
-You broke my heart-

I watched your life unfold
From afar
Every blessing, a new wound to scar
I tried to tell you that I missed the mark
-A wildfire in my life from a single spark-

We both had to start again
Moving through what could have been
Letting go
Instead of Reaching in
-I dream of you at the days' end-

Good Knight

Good night, sir __ __
Knight of great cause
Slayer of demons
And bringer of stars
Good night to the day
With whom you've travelled so far
Rest here near Heaven
On a cloud called my heart

No Cilantro

Cute socks
Walks in the dark
Say you're gonna love me
And won't ever stop

Sushi dates
And textin' late
Say you're gonna keep me
Cause you know it's fate

Sunset nights
Watching city lights
Say you're gonna stay with me
Cause it's feeling right

Tacos
No cilantro
Take my picture
But don't let me go

Dinner parties
Just your friends and me
10,000 faces
But it's you I see

Daytime dancing
Swimming in the sea
Say you're gonna live with me
Here's my heart and take the key

Bird watching
With the dog makes three
Say you're gonna make it real
Will you marry me

Sunlight
Waking up in peace
Say you're gonna kiss me
This was meant to be

Your Ocean

Like a wave you wash over me
Your tide pulling at my heartstrings
Catch a breath before you pull me under
Will I ever come back up
　　Is what I wonder
Am I lost out to sea in your ocean
Body's moving but I can't find the motions
Head is spinning and I'm dreaming that it's not real
If it's not real, then how come it's all I feel

You are all
　　Around me
Waking me from my sleep
Kissing every part of me
Two souls anchored deep
Another life, you're choosing me

Cast ashore on the island of your heart
I feel your presence but the light here
　　It went dark
Looking up now, nighttime, at the stars
Say a prayer
And hope that it travels far
Castaway out to sea in your ocean

Mind is racing yet I'm out of emotions
Love is waiting but I'm sensing that it's not real
If it's not real, then how come it's all I feel

You are all
            Around me
Waking me from my sleep
Kissing every part of me
Two souls drifting free
Another life, it's meant to be

The Boy in the Box in the Stars

I drove all night in the dark
Through the sunset
And straight past Mars
I drove this way and that way
To get to you
An intergalactic highway
Mapped from memories I drew

I left behind all the people
Giving lectures and sidebars
Crossed out all the poems
Burned the books and the memoirs

I kept driving and driving
A desert of space
While the records kept playing
And the future gave chase
Finally I found you in a place that was ours
The boy in the box
A glass house in the stars

Halfway

Rest here on my shoulder friend
Halfway between the head and the heart
Somewhere between the middle and the start
Tomorrow will send us going apart
The journey keeps going
The ending is far

Almost Love

You know it could have been you
The one right from the start
It's been seven thousand days
And look where we are, we barely even talk

I thought I told you the truth
That I felt tossed out and used
Love was out of reach
But I hope you know, it was never you

Somehow this is what's it's come to
Reaching through the phone
Thinking 'bout the old times
Almost love don't ya know

You know I'm jaded
Stuck on your face
Knowing I got to give up on the chase
So I've settled down
Guess what, it's love I've found
And I hope that we can stay friends
It's been all this time
You know I keep you close
Almost love on my mind